Meta's Orion Smart Glasses

The Future of Mobile Computing Right Before Your Eyes

How Augmented Reality is Set to Replace Smartphones and Redefine Our Digital World

Kylan P.crook

Copyright © 2024 by Kylan P.crook

All rights reserved. This book is an original work and copyrighted publication, protected under the laws of the United kingdom. No part of this book, including its content or any other material, may be reproduced or transmitted in any form or by any means, including photocopying, recording, or other electronic or mechanical methods without the prior written permission of the copyright owner. The information provided in this book is intended for personal use and educational purposes only.

TABLE OF CONTENT

INTRODUCTION.. 3
Chapter 1: A Brief History of Smart Glasses and AR Technology... 7
Chapter 2: The Design Breakthrough: Sleek, Stylish, and Ready for Daily Use........................ 15
Chapter 3: Inside the Tech: How Orion Makes AR Immersive... 24
Chapter 4: Gesture Control and Voice Commands: A New Way to Interact................... 34
Chapter 5: The Power of Meta AI: More Than Just a Gadget.. 43
Chapter 6: Battery Life and Portability: Can Orion Truly Replace Smartphones?.................. 52
Chapter 7: Privacy and Security: The Double-Edged Sword of AR Glasses................ 61
Chapter 8: Competing with Giants: How Orion Stacks Up Against Apple, Microsoft, and Google... 71
Chapter 9: Beyond the Consumer Market: Orion's Potential in Industry and Education.... 81
Chapter 10: The Future of Smart Glasses: Where Do We Go from Here?........................... 92
CONCLUSION... 102
    The Beginning of a New Era.................... 102

INTRODUCTION

The Next Revolution in Mobile Computing

Brief overview of the history of smart glasses and AR technology.
In recent years, the concept of augmented reality (AR) has moved from the fringes of science fiction into mainstream technology. At the heart of this transformation are smart glasses, devices designed to overlay digital information onto the real world, merging both into one seamless experience. The earliest iterations of AR glasses, like Google Glass, Microsoft's HoloLens, and Magic Leap, showed promise, but each faced limitations that prevented widespread adoption. Privacy concerns, bulky designs, and high costs made these products niche rather than revolutionary.

Yet, with technological advances, the possibility of AR glasses becoming a part of everyday life has steadily grown.

This is where Meta, the company behind social media platforms like Facebook, Instagram, and WhatsApp, steps in with its Orion Smart Glasses. Having invested heavily in virtual reality (VR) through its Oculus brand, Meta is no stranger to immersive technologies. Now, with Orion, Meta aims to redefine how we interact with digital content by integrating AR into a device that could one day replace the smartphone. The significance of this shift cannot be overstated—smartphones are our primary tool for communication, entertainment, and navigation in the modern world. Meta's bold vision is to place that entire experience, and more, right in front of our eyes.

What makes the idea of AR replacing smartphones so significant? The potential is immense. Imagine a world where instead of looking down at a screen, the information you need is displayed seamlessly in your field of vision. Navigation instructions appear as overlays on the road while walking or driving, messages pop up directly in your line of sight, and video calls feel more immersive, as the person you're speaking with appears as a hologram in your environment. All of this allows for a hands-free, more integrated way of interacting with the digital world, fundamentally changing how we relate to technology in our daily lives.

Meta's Orion Smart Glasses are poised to do more than just provide convenience—they have the potential to transform industries, entertainment, education, and even healthcare. The promise of AR is no longer about isolated gimmicks; it's about reshaping how we perceive and engage with the world around us. With Meta's expertise in creating social platforms that connect billions of people, Orion could become the device that turns AR into a mainstream, everyday tool. The question is not just whether the technology can succeed, but how soon we will begin to see its effects in our daily routines.

Chapter 1: A Brief History of Smart Glasses and AR Technology

Smart glasses and augmented reality (AR) technology have been part of the tech conversation for over a decade, but their journey has been marked by several missteps and challenges. **Google Glass**, introduced in 2013, was one of the earliest attempts to bring AR technology to the mainstream. It promised a futuristic experience where users could access information through a transparent display integrated into their eyeglasses. The idea of having navigation, messages, and video calls in front of your eyes seemed revolutionary. However, the product struggled to take off.

Its design, although cutting-edge at the time, was bulky and awkward for everyday wear. More importantly, privacy concerns quickly surfaced. With a camera constantly recording the user's surroundings, people were wary of potential surveillance issues, leading to widespread criticism. These concerns, paired with its high cost, meant Google Glass failed to capture a mass market.

Microsoft's HoloLens, which followed, took a different approach. Released in 2016, it was a more advanced device, aimed at enterprise users rather than everyday consumers. HoloLens offered mixed reality capabilities, blending real-world environments with digital overlays in a way that could revolutionize industries like healthcare, engineering, and design. However, its price point—much higher than that of Google Glass—along with its bulkiness, made it impractical for general consumers. While it found success in niche markets and professional settings, it did little to push AR technology into the hands of the average person.

Microsoft's focus on business applications rather than the consumer market was a clear indication that AR glasses still had a long way to go before replacing smartphones.

Another significant player in the AR space was **Magic Leap**, a company that raised billions of dollars in funding and generated immense hype for its AR glasses. The Magic Leap One, released in 2018, was marketed as a revolutionary step in AR technology, with the potential to transform entertainment and digital interaction. However, it ultimately fell short of expectations. The device was once again bulky, expensive, and targeted at developers and enterprise users rather than the general public.

Magic Leap's vision of a world where digital elements could seamlessly integrate with the real world was ambitious, but the technology wasn't quite ready for consumer use. Despite being more advanced than its predecessors,

Magic Leap's product was too niche and costly to gain widespread adoption.

The **challenges faced by these early AR glasses**—privacy concerns, bulky designs, and niche markets—set the stage for a slow adoption of the technology. Privacy, in particular, remained a persistent issue. With AR glasses constantly capturing video, users and bystanders alike were concerned about being recorded without their consent. This concern was compounded by the fact that most early AR glasses had visible cameras, making them feel invasive. Another major barrier was the **design** of these devices.

Consumers were not willing to wear something bulky and obviously technological on their faces all day, especially when the benefits of doing so were not immediately clear. The lack of a truly seamless, stylish design meant that AR glasses couldn't compete with the sleek, portable convenience of smartphones. Finally, the **niche markets** these products targeted further limited their appeal. By focusing on enterprise or developer markets, companies like Microsoft and Magic Leap missed the opportunity to capture the attention of everyday consumers.

Despite the hype around each of these products, **AR glasses haven't yet replaced smartphones**, and there are several reasons for this. First and foremost, smartphones are incredibly versatile devices that offer everything from communication to entertainment, all in a compact and portable form. While AR glasses promised to overlay digital content onto the real world, they often required users to carry additional equipment, such as external computing units or bulky batteries, making them far less convenient than smartphones.

Furthermore, the lack of essential apps and services available on these AR platforms made them less practical. A phone that fits into your pocket and allows you to access any service you need is far more appealing than an AR device that can only do a few specialized tasks.

Moreover, the **user experience** was often clunky, with limited fields of view and awkward input methods. Unlike a smartphone, which you can control with the tap of a finger, early AR glasses required voice commands, hand gestures, or even external controllers, making them less intuitive. Without a smooth, integrated user experience, AR glasses struggled to compete in a world where smartphones were the ultimate all-in-one device.

This is where **Meta** entered the picture. Having made significant investments in virtual reality through **Oculus**, Meta began positioning itself as a leader in immersive technologies. Oculus gave the company valuable experience in developing advanced headsets and creating engaging digital environments. However, virtual reality had its limitations—it was primarily suited for gaming and entertainment, rather than everyday use. Meta realized that augmented reality, which blends the digital and physical worlds, had the potential to become much more ubiquitous. By applying the lessons learned from Oculus, Meta began to focus on developing AR technologies that could eventually replace smartphones.

The launch of **Meta's Orion Smart Glasses** represents a major step in this progression. Meta's vision for Orion is to offer an AR experience that is lightweight, stylish, and practical for everyday use. Unlike its predecessors, which were often bulky and designed for niche markets, Orion aims to appeal to a broad audience, with a design that resembles regular glasses. Meta is betting that by improving the design and integrating advanced features like voice commands and gesture controls, they can finally make AR glasses a viable alternative to smartphones.

The transition from Oculus to Orion also reflects Meta's broader ambitions in the AR and VR space. While VR remains a key part of the company's strategy, AR offers more immediate applications for everyday life, making it the ideal platform for a potential smartphone replacement.

Meta's development of Orion is not just about creating a better AR device—it's about fundamentally changing how we interact with technology. By reducing the reliance on smartphones and bringing digital content into the real world, Meta hopes to lead the charge into a new era of computing. Whether they can succeed where others have failed remains to be seen, but the company's focus on refining the design, improving the user experience, and addressing privacy concerns shows that they are serious about making AR glasses the next big thing in tech.

Chapter 2: The Design Breakthrough: Sleek, Stylish, and Ready for Daily Use

When it comes to wearable technology, **design is everything**. For smart glasses, this is especially true, as they need to balance functionality with the aesthetic appeal that makes them comfortable and stylish for daily use. Meta's **Orion Smart Glasses** are a bold attempt to do just that, aiming to succeed where previous augmented reality (AR) glasses have struggled. One of the most impressive aspects of Orion is Meta's focus on making the device lightweight, coming in at under **100 grams**.

This is a significant achievement, particularly when compared to earlier AR devices like Magic Leap, which weigh over **250 grams**. Magic Leap's bulky design contributed to its limited appeal; users found the device too heavy and awkward to wear for extended periods. Meta is clearly aware of these limitations and has made it a priority to create a product that feels as much like regular eyewear as possible.

The reduced weight of **Orion** is more than just a matter of comfort. For AR glasses to truly replace smartphones, they need to be something users can wear all day, without feeling like they have a piece of advanced tech strapped to their faces. This means that not only does the weight matter, but the overall design must blend seamlessly with everyday life. Meta has taken strides to make Orion's design sleeker than previous AR devices, avoiding the clunky, sci-fi look that plagued earlier models.

The goal is to create something that feels natural—a pair of glasses that you wouldn't mind wearing out to dinner, to a meeting, or while running errands.

However, **balancing functionality with style** in the world of AR technology is no easy task.

While Meta has certainly made improvements in terms of weight and appearance, Orion still faces the challenge of whether it's truly ready to replace regular glasses. The device consists of three key components: the glasses themselves, an external computing unit that fits into the user's pocket, and an electromyography (EMG) wristband used for input. While these components work together to keep the glasses lightweight, the reliance on additional devices—particularly the external computing unit—raises questions about whether Orion is convenient enough for daily, widespread use.

Smartphones, after all, pack all their necessary technology into a single, compact device. To truly replace smartphones, Orion will need to streamline its functionality without requiring users to carry around extra pieces of hardware.

The design of the glasses themselves is sleek by AR standards, but there are still noticeable **tech elements** that distinguish them from regular eyewear. For instance, while Meta has made the frames as thin as possible, they are still visibly thicker than typical glasses.

This is because the frames house some of the technology that powers the AR experience, including sensors, cameras, and display mechanisms. This creates a trade-off: while the design is sleeker than previous models, the glasses still don't quite pass for something you would pick up at an optical store. Meta is betting that users will be willing to accept these design quirks in exchange for the advanced functionality that Orion offers, but it remains to be seen whether this balance is enough to convince the average consumer.

Another **challenge with miniaturization** is ensuring that the glasses remain comfortable while incorporating all the necessary technology. AR devices require a considerable amount of computing power to function properly, and squeezing this technology into a device as small as a pair of glasses is no small feat.

While Meta has managed to keep Orion relatively lightweight, the inclusion of cameras, sensors, and display systems means that the frames are still thicker than what most people are used to wearing. For many potential users, these visible tech elements might be a dealbreaker, as they still carry the stigma of being too futuristic or out of place in everyday life.

Despite these challenges, Meta's design choices represent a significant improvement over its competitors. **Magic Leap's AR glasses**, for example, are not only heavier but also feature a more conspicuous design. The bulky headsets of Magic Leap and Microsoft's HoloLens are a far cry from the sleek, almost regular appearance of Orion. While these competitors have focused on enterprise markets—where design aesthetics are less of a priority—Meta is aiming directly at the consumer market, where style and comfort are critical factors for success. By keeping the glasses under 100 grams and focusing on a stylish appearance, Meta is positioning Orion as a product that users can integrate into their everyday lives, rather than a piece of specialized technology reserved for niche applications.

One of the key questions that remains is whether Orion's design can truly pass for **everyday eyewear**. While the glasses are certainly lighter and more comfortable than previous AR devices, they are still noticeably tech-infused, with visible sensors and thicker frames. This raises the question of whether consumers will be willing to wear them in public. Meta has made significant strides in improving the design, but for Orion to replace smartphones, it will need to become something that users feel comfortable wearing in all settings—not just tech-savvy environments or for specific tasks.

Beyond aesthetics, the design of Orion also presents technical challenges that impact its functionality. **Miniaturization** is crucial for keeping the glasses lightweight and stylish, but it also limits the amount of technology that can be packed into the device. This is where the external computing unit comes into play. By offloading some of the processing power to a unit that fits into the user's pocket, Meta has managed to keep the glasses themselves relatively slim.

However, this approach introduces a level of complexity that smartphones don't have. With a smartphone, all the necessary components are integrated into one device, making it easy to carry and use. Orion's reliance on an external computing unit, while innovative, may hinder its appeal as a true smartphone replacement. For users who prioritize convenience, the need to carry an additional piece of hardware may be a significant drawback.

Meta's design team is undoubtedly aware of these challenges, and they have made it clear that **future iterations** of Orion will aim to improve on the current model. The goal is to make the glasses even lighter and more discreet, further blurring the line between regular eyewear and AR devices. As technology advances and miniaturization becomes more sophisticated, it's likely that we'll see future versions of Orion that are even closer to resembling the glasses we're used to wearing. For now, though, the design of Orion represents a promising step forward in the evolution of AR glasses—offering a balance between functionality and style that is closer than ever to being practical for everyday use.

Meta's focus on design is not just about making a visually appealing product; it's about **changing how we interact with technology**. By creating a device that feels comfortable and stylish enough to wear every day, Meta is pushing the boundaries of what AR glasses can be. Whether Orion can fully replace smartphones remains to be seen, but the progress made in design is an essential part of making that vision a reality. As AR technology continues to evolve, Meta's Orion Smart Glasses may very well be the first step toward a future where our digital world is seamlessly integrated with the real one, and we no longer rely on the devices in our pockets to stay connected.

Chapter 3: Inside the Tech: How Orion Makes AR Immersive

The success of any augmented reality (AR) device lies in its ability to immerse users in a digital experience that feels natural and unobtrusive. Meta's **Orion Smart Glasses** have taken significant strides in achieving this level of immersion, and much of it stems from the technology built into the device. One of the most notable features of Orion is its **70-degree field of view**, a key improvement over previous AR glasses. Most AR devices on the market suffer from limited fields of view, which create a restrictive experience.

When digital elements are only visible in a narrow window, the illusion of AR breaks, and the technology feels less integrated with the real world. Meta's choice to expand the field of view to 70 degrees is crucial, as it allows for a wider range of digital content to be displayed, creating a more immersive and seamless interaction between the user and their surroundings.

A larger field of view means that **digital elements**—whether they be navigation directions, video calls, or notifications—are more naturally integrated into the user's line of sight. Instead of feeling as if you're looking through a narrow portal into the digital world, Orion's display allows users to feel as though the digital content is genuinely part of their environment. This **blending of digital and real-world elements** is what makes AR so compelling, and it's what Orion does better than most of its competitors.

By expanding the field of view, Meta has ensured that users won't feel constrained or limited by the technology, which helps maintain the illusion of AR and makes the overall experience feel more natural.

Behind this immersive experience is **Orion's display technology**, which is designed to project digital images with stunning clarity and precision. The display system overlays holographic images onto the real world without distorting the user's perception of their surroundings. This is a critical element of AR—the digital images must feel integrated rather than superimposed. Orion's display ensures that digital content is crisp and clear, even when viewed in conjunction with real-world elements. This is particularly important for tasks that require precision, such as following navigation directions or interacting with complex digital interfaces.

The **components** of the Orion system are what enable this seamless experience. The glasses themselves are equipped with advanced display technology, sensors, and cameras that track the user's environment and movements.

However, unlike many other AR devices, which attempt to pack all of the necessary technology into the glasses, Orion relies on an **external computing unit**.

This external unit, which fits into the user's pocket, handles much of the heavy processing required to run the AR experience. By offloading the computational tasks to an external device, Meta has been able to keep the glasses themselves lightweight, making them more comfortable for extended wear. This approach is one of the reasons why Orion weighs less than 100 grams, a significant improvement over earlier, bulkier AR devices.

The use of an **external computing unit** has its advantages, but it also introduces a layer of complexity for users. On the one hand, the external unit allows the glasses to remain lightweight and stylish, which is crucial for making AR glasses appealing to everyday users. On the other hand, the need to carry an additional piece of hardware may detract from the convenience that AR glasses are supposed to offer. For users who are used to the all-in-one functionality of smartphones, the idea of carrying a separate device for processing power could be seen as a drawback. Meta's challenge is to make this trade-off feel worthwhile by ensuring that the enhanced AR experience outweighs the inconvenience of carrying an external unit.

Another critical component of the Orion system is the **EMG wristband**, which is used for input. Traditional AR glasses have relied on a combination of voice commands, hand gestures, or external controllers to allow users to interact with digital content. While these methods work, they often feel clunky and unnatural. Meta's solution is the electromyography (EMG) wristband, which detects even the smallest muscle movements in the user's wrist and translates them into digital commands.

This allows for more intuitive and precise control over the AR interface. For example, a pinching motion can be used to select an item, while a swiping gesture can scroll through a menu. The result is an input method that feels more fluid and responsive than the voice or gesture-based systems used by previous AR devices.

By integrating the EMG wristband with the glasses and the external computing unit, Meta has created a **system** that allows users to interact with AR in a way that feels more natural and less cumbersome. The wristband eliminates the need for external controllers or exaggerated hand gestures, making the user's interactions with the digital world more subtle and integrated. This, in turn, enhances the immersive experience that Orion aims to provide.

The more natural the input methods, the less aware the user becomes of the technology itself, allowing them to focus on the content and interactions rather than the device.

While the **external computing unit** is what enables the glasses to remain lightweight, it does come with its own set of challenges. One of the main issues is that it introduces an additional piece of hardware that users need to manage. Unlike smartphones, which are self-contained devices, Orion requires users to carry not only the glasses but also the external unit. This could be seen as a step backward in terms of convenience, especially for users who value the portability and simplicity of their current devices.

The external unit is designed to be discreet and portable, but the fact remains that it adds an extra layer of complexity to the user's experience. Meta's goal is to minimize this complexity as much as possible, but for some users, the need to carry multiple components may detract from the overall appeal of the device.

Despite these challenges, the **benefits** of the external unit are clear. By handling the processing power outside of the glasses themselves, Meta has been able to make the glasses significantly lighter and more comfortable to wear.

This is a critical factor in making AR glasses viable for daily use. Previous AR devices, such as Magic Leap, struggled with bulkiness and weight, making them impractical for long-term wear. Orion's lightweight design is a direct result of the decision to offload processing power to an external unit, and this trade-off may ultimately be worth it for users who prioritize comfort and style.

In the long term, Meta will likely continue to refine this system, with future versions of Orion potentially integrating more of the technology into the glasses themselves. **Miniaturization** will be key to achieving this, as Meta strives to make AR glasses that are not only powerful but also convenient and user-friendly. For now, the external computing unit represents a clever solution to the problem of balancing power with portability, allowing Meta to deliver an immersive AR experience without sacrificing the comfort and wearability of the glasses.

Ultimately, Orion's ability to create an immersive AR experience relies on the **synergy** between its components. The 70-degree field of view, the high-quality display, the external computing unit, and the EMG wristband all work together to deliver an experience that feels seamless and natural. The technology fades into the background, allowing users to focus on the content and interactions, rather than the device itself. This is the goal of any successful AR device—to make the technology feel invisible so that the experience becomes the primary focus.

Orion is well on its way to achieving this, and as Meta continues to refine the system, we may see even more immersive and integrated AR experiences in the near future.

Chapter 4: Gesture Control and Voice Commands: A New Way to Interact

The way we interact with technology has evolved dramatically over the years, from physical keyboards to touchscreens, and now, with the advent of augmented reality, we are moving toward even more intuitive forms of interaction. Meta's **Orion Smart Glasses** push this evolution further by introducing a combination of **gesture control** and **voice commands**, redefining how users engage with digital content in the real world. One of the most innovative aspects of Orion is its **EMG wristband**, which enables users to control the AR interface through subtle gestures.

This system takes interactivity beyond the simple tapping and swiping motions of a smartphone, offering a more fluid, immersive way to manipulate digital objects within the AR space.

At the heart of this new interaction method is the **electromyography (EMG) wristband**. This wristband is capable of detecting even the smallest muscle movements in the user's wrist and translating them into digital commands. Unlike earlier AR systems that relied on large, exaggerated hand gestures or cumbersome external controllers, the EMG wristband makes control seamless and nearly invisible. A simple **pinching motion** with your fingers can be used to select items, while a subtle **swiping movement** with your hand can scroll through menus or pages of content.

This makes interactions feel much more natural, as users are not required to make large, attention-drawing gestures to navigate the AR interface.

The beauty of this system is its subtlety. For example, imagine browsing through a selection of apps or messages in your AR interface while walking down the street. With the EMG wristband, there's no need to stop, reach for your device, or even look down at a screen.

Instead, by simply making a small pinching gesture, you can open an app, and a quick swipe can move you through the content. The **user experience** becomes fluid and continuous, allowing for a level of multitasking and interaction that's nearly impossible with traditional devices like smartphones. By allowing users to engage with the AR interface using only subtle muscle movements, Meta's Orion Smart Glasses create a user experience that feels integrated into the flow of daily life, rather than interrupting it.

In addition to gesture control, Meta has integrated **voice commands** into the Orion system, leveraging the power of Meta's AI to create a hands-free interaction experience.

Voice commands have been a popular feature in modern devices for some time, but their integration into the AR environment takes them to a new level. With Orion, users can perform a wide variety of tasks simply by speaking, all without needing to touch the device or perform physical gestures. This enhances the hands-free nature of AR, making it even more practical for everyday use, whether you're driving, cooking, or simply don't want to stop what you're doing to interact with your technology.

Meta's AI plays a critical role in making **voice command functionality** as natural and responsive as possible. The AI is designed to understand and process **natural language**, meaning that users don't need to memorize specific commands or phrases. Instead, they can speak to Orion as they would to another person. For example, you might say, "Call John," or "Show me the weather for tomorrow," and Orion will respond accordingly. The AI processes the request and executes it in real-time, displaying the necessary information in the user's field of vision. This hands-free interaction transforms Orion from just another gadget into something more akin to a **personal assistant**, capable of helping users with a wide range of tasks, all through voice interaction.

The ability to use **voice commands** is particularly useful in situations where gestures might not be practical or convenient. For instance, if you're driving and need to send a quick message, simply speaking to Orion can get the task done without having to take your hands off the wheel or your eyes off the road. Likewise, in a kitchen setting, you could ask Orion to play a recipe video or set a timer while your hands are busy.

The flexibility and versatility that voice commands offer make the glasses even more functional and easy to integrate into different aspects of life.

What makes Orion's voice commands even more impressive is the **integration of Meta's AI** with the AR interface.

The AI not only understands what you're asking for but also takes into account your surroundings, offering contextual information that enhances the AR experience. For example, if you're in a new city and ask for directions, the AI can overlay navigation directly onto the streets in front of you, providing step-by-step guidance that feels more immersive than simply following a map on a phone. Similarly, if you're at home and ask Orion to find information online, it can pull up content in your field of view, allowing you to continue whatever you're doing without interruption.

The combination of **gesture control and voice commands** represents a significant leap forward in how we interact with AR devices. With previous technology, controlling AR required cumbersome setups—external controllers, exaggerated gestures, or clunky user interfaces that felt disconnected from the real world. Meta's approach with Orion is to make interaction as seamless and natural as possible, so the user feels like the technology is part of their everyday life rather than a novelty.

The **EMG wristband** allows for precise, subtle control of the digital environment, while the **voice command functionality**, powered by Meta's AI, ensures that users can interact with Orion without needing to use their hands at all. These features together create an interface that feels intuitive and user-friendly, paving the way for a new era of AR interaction.

What makes Orion stand out in this realm is its ability to **blend physical and digital interactions** so smoothly. Rather than forcing users to adapt to new, awkward ways of controlling their devices, Orion adapts to how people naturally move and communicate. The EMG wristband, with its ability to detect tiny muscle movements, enables users to interact with digital elements without drawing attention to themselves, a critical factor in making AR glasses feel integrated into daily life rather than a futuristic gimmick. The wristband essentially becomes an extension of the user's body, allowing for effortless interaction with digital content in a way that doesn't disrupt the flow of regular activities.

Moreover, the **voice command system** makes Orion feel much more than just a pair of AR glasses. With the AI's ability to handle complex requests, retrieve information, and offer contextual guidance, the glasses become a digital assistant that is constantly available, listening, and ready to assist. By integrating this level of functionality, Meta has positioned Orion as not just a tool for AR enthusiasts or tech-savvy individuals but as a product that could potentially appeal to a broader consumer base.

The hands-free capabilities make it especially useful for people who are always on the go or have jobs that require multitasking, from professionals in the field to parents managing household tasks.

In conclusion, Meta's approach to interaction with Orion represents a major leap in usability for AR devices. The **gesture control system**, powered by the EMG wristband, offers precision and subtlety that previous AR devices lacked. The ability to control the AR interface through small, natural movements means users can engage with digital content without interrupting their daily activities. Coupled with the **voice command functionality**, which leverages the power of Meta's AI, Orion offers an unparalleled hands-free experience, making it feel like a true digital assistant rather than just another piece of tech.

This seamless integration of physical gestures and voice commands sets the stage for a future where AR glasses are not only useful but also essential tools for navigating and interacting with our increasingly digital world.

Chapter 5: The Power of Meta AI: More Than Just a Gadget

Meta's **Orion Smart Glasses** are more than just a piece of hardware designed to bring augmented reality (AR) into everyday life. What sets Orion apart from other AR devices is its seamless integration with **Meta AI**, a powerful artificial intelligence system that acts as the brains behind the operation. Meta AI transforms the glasses from a simple display of digital overlays into an intelligent, responsive tool that can anticipate user needs, provide real-time contextual information, and automate daily tasks with ease.

This integration makes Orion much more than a wearable gadget—it positions the device as a potential **AI assistant**, capable of reshaping how we interact with the world.

At the core of this transformation is how **Meta AI integrates with Orion** to deliver real-time information that is not only relevant but also contextually aware.

The AI system constantly processes the environment around the user, using cameras and sensors embedded in the glasses to understand their surroundings. This allows Meta AI to provide information that is directly applicable to the user's current situation. For example, if a user is walking down the street and asks for nearby restaurants, Meta AI can instantly pull up a list of options, displaying them as holograms in the user's field of view, complete with directions and reviews.

This kind of **contextual awareness** creates a more immersive and practical AR experience, as users no longer have to switch between looking at their phones and their surroundings. Instead, everything they need to know is right in front of them, blended seamlessly with the real world.

One of the most exciting aspects of this AI integration is its ability to **identify objects** in the user's environment. Imagine wearing Orion and walking through a park.

With a simple voice command, you could ask Meta AI to identify a tree or a landmark, and the glasses would instantly display relevant information, such as the type of tree or the history of the landmark. This capability makes Orion not just a tool for displaying information but a gateway to a deeper understanding of the world around us. It also opens up new possibilities for education, tourism, and even professional use in fields like architecture, where real-time identification and information about buildings or materials could be invaluable.

Another powerful capability of **Meta AI** is its ability to provide **navigation assistance** in real-time. Whether you're driving or walking, Orion can overlay navigation directions directly onto the streets in front of you, making it easier than ever to get from one place to another without constantly glancing down at your phone. The AI processes your location, the surrounding streets, and even traffic conditions to give you the most efficient route. This level of **hands-free navigation** is not only convenient but also safer, as it allows users to keep their attention on the road or their surroundings rather than on a screen.

Beyond object identification and navigation, **Meta AI excels at automating daily tasks**. The AI system is designed to handle a wide range of activities that we currently perform on our smartphones, but with the added convenience of **hands-free operation**. With voice command-driven tasks, users can make calls, send messages, browse the internet, check emails, or even start a video call, all without needing to touch the device.

This creates a **personal assistant-like experience**, where the user can delegate tasks to the AI while continuing to go about their day.

For instance, while preparing breakfast in the kitchen, you could ask Orion to send a message to a colleague or check the weather forecast, all while keeping your hands free to finish cooking. Similarly, in a professional setting, you could use Orion to quickly schedule meetings, respond to emails, or pull up important documents without having to stop what you're doing. The integration of **voice commands** and **AI-driven automation** streamlines daily tasks in a way that no smartphone can match. It frees up time and mental energy by allowing users to offload routine activities onto the AI, making Orion a practical tool for both personal and professional use.

The power of **Meta AI** becomes even more apparent when you consider its potential to

evolve beyond its current capabilities. Right now, Meta AI acts as an intelligent assistant that responds to user commands and delivers contextual information.

However, as artificial intelligence technology continues to advance, Orion could become much more than just an AR device. Meta AI has the potential to **anticipate user needs** before they are even expressed. For example, if the AI notices that you are frequently visiting a particular location or searching for similar types of information, it could start suggesting relevant content or actions proactively. This kind of predictive capability would make Orion feel even more like a true **AI assistant**, one that not only responds to commands but also enhances the user's life by making helpful suggestions and taking initiative.

The future of Orion as a **personal AI assistant** also holds exciting possibilities for **deep personalization**. Meta AI could learn a user's preferences, habits, and routines, tailoring its interactions and suggestions based on this knowledge. Imagine an AI assistant that knows when you prefer to exercise, what types of restaurants you enjoy, or when you typically schedule meetings. This level of personalization could create a truly customized AR experience, where the digital world adapts to your specific needs and preferences, enhancing your day-to-day life in meaningful ways.

Moreover, as **Meta AI evolves**, it could also start integrating more advanced capabilities like **natural language processing** and **machine learning**. This would allow the AI to understand more complex user requests and engage in deeper, more nuanced conversations. Instead of just giving basic responses, Meta AI could start offering more thoughtful insights or even help with decision-making processes. For instance, if a user asks for advice on a restaurant or an upcoming trip, Meta AI could offer detailed suggestions based on past preferences, reviews, and current trends, making the AI an invaluable resource for both personal and professional decision-making.

Looking even further into the future, there is the potential for **Meta AI** to play a pivotal role in **augmented reality-enhanced social interactions**. Imagine having a conversation with a friend while Orion enhances the experience by displaying real-time information about shared memories, places you've visited together, or even upcoming events you're both interested in. Meta AI could help facilitate deeper connections by making relevant information readily available during social interactions, enriching the conversation without being intrusive.

The potential for **Orion** to evolve into a true AI assistant is vast. While the device currently excels at providing real-time contextual information, object identification, and task automation, it is clear that Meta has bigger ambitions for the future of this technology.

As AI continues to advance, Orion could transform from an AR gadget into an essential, personalized tool that assists users in every aspect of their lives, anticipating needs, automating tasks, and providing invaluable insights in real time. This evolution would mark a significant shift in how we think about wearable technology—not just as a means of consuming digital content but as a fully integrated part of how we navigate and interact with the world.

In essence, **Meta AI** elevates **Orion Smart Glasses** from a simple AR device to a powerful assistant that can help users navigate the complexities of daily life with ease. By combining real-time contextual information with hands-free task automation, Meta AI turns Orion into more than just a gadget—it becomes a tool that anticipates and enhances the user's experiences, making it an indispensable part of the future of augmented reality and personal technology.

Chapter 6: Battery Life and Portability: Can Orion Truly Replace Smartphones?

One of the most critical factors in determining whether **Meta's Orion Smart Glasses** can truly replace smartphones is **battery life**. For any wearable device to become a daily essential, it needs to offer reliable, long-lasting power. Yet, this has been a significant hurdle for most augmented reality (AR) devices, and Orion is no exception. The level of **computational power** required to run an immersive AR experience—combined with real-time sensors, displays, and the external computing unit—places considerable demands on the battery.

As a result, many AR glasses, including Orion, have limited battery life, often lasting only a few hours before needing a recharge. This limitation raises questions about how practical it is for Orion to function as a **smartphone replacement**.

A smartphone's battery is designed to last a full day with moderate use, and users have grown accustomed to this convenience. The problem with AR devices like Orion is that the more immersive and advanced the technology becomes, the more power it requires. Orion's **70-degree field of view**, high-quality holographic display, constant environmental tracking, and the ability to handle tasks such as messaging, browsing, and video calls demand far more energy than the average smartphone.

Even with its **external computing unit**, which handles much of the processing power, the device still struggles to maintain enough battery life for prolonged use. For now, the reality is that Orion likely won't be able to last an entire day on a single charge, especially with intensive tasks such as continuous navigation or video calls.

The **external computing unit** that Meta has included with Orion is a clever solution to some of the challenges of battery life and performance. By moving much of the processing power outside of the glasses themselves, Meta has been able to keep the glasses lightweight and relatively sleek, avoiding the bulky, uncomfortable designs that plagued earlier AR devices. However, this external unit introduces a **new layer of complexity** in terms of portability. Users must now carry an additional piece of hardware, which, while small enough to fit in a pocket, still detracts from the streamlined, all-in-one experience that smartphones offer.

In terms of **mobility and convenience**, this raises an important question: **Is carrying an external computing unit a step backward for mobile computing?** For many users, the appeal of a smartphone lies in its

simplicity—one device that can do everything, with no need for extra accessories or hardware.

The idea of carrying around a separate unit for Orion, no matter how small or discreet, adds complexity to what is supposed to be an everyday, wearable device. This could be seen as a significant drawback, especially for users who prioritize convenience and portability in their technology. After all, a smartphone fits easily into a pocket or bag, offering instant access to a world of digital content without the need for additional components.

Moreover, the **external computing unit** impacts the overall **user experience** in subtle ways. While it certainly helps extend the battery life and processing power of the glasses, it also means that users must be mindful of two devices instead of one. There's the possibility of forgetting or misplacing the unit, and the added responsibility of ensuring that both the glasses and the unit are charged and functioning properly.

For individuals used to the seamless, integrated nature of a smartphone, this could feel like an unnecessary complication.

That said, the use of an external unit does allow **Orion** to perform at a higher level than if all the components were housed within the glasses. By offloading some of the more energy-intensive tasks to the external unit, Meta has been able to make **significant advances** in AR technology without sacrificing too much in terms of weight or comfort. In this sense, the trade-off between carrying an external unit and enjoying a more powerful AR experience might be worth it for users who are willing to embrace this new form of mobile computing.

However, for Orion to truly replace smartphones, **future models** will need to address some of these issues. One area of potential improvement is in making the glasses more **self-contained**, reducing or even eliminating the need for an external computing unit. As technology continues to advance, it's likely that we will see more **miniaturization** of key components, allowing for more powerful processors and longer-lasting batteries to be integrated directly into the glasses themselves. This would not only make the device more convenient to carry and use but would also bring it closer to the ideal of a **true smartphone replacement**—a single device that does everything without the need for extra hardware.

Additionally, improvements in **battery technology** could help solve one of the most pressing issues for Orion and other AR devices. Advances in areas such as **solid-state batteries** or **wireless charging** could extend the device's lifespan between charges, making it more viable for all-day use. For example, wireless charging solutions embedded in everyday objects—such as charging surfaces in cars, desks, or even public spaces—could allow users to recharge their Orion glasses throughout the day without needing to plug them in. This would go a long way toward addressing the current limitations of battery life, allowing users to wear their glasses for longer periods without interruption.

Another potential area for improvement lies in **software optimization**. By refining the algorithms that manage power consumption, Meta could extend Orion's battery life without needing to rely solely on hardware advancements. Efficient software that prioritizes low-power operations when the device is not in heavy use could help conserve battery life, ensuring that users get more time out of each charge. These software-based improvements could make a significant difference in the **overall user experience**, allowing for a smoother, more reliable AR experience without sacrificing battery life.

In terms of **long-term potential**, Orion has a clear path to becoming more self-sufficient and streamlined, but it's going to take **multiple**

iterations of the product to get there. The first versions of the glasses, including the current model, will likely rely on external units to handle processing and extend battery life. However, as Meta continues to invest in AR technology and push the boundaries of what's possible, it's reasonable to expect that future versions of Orion will become more self-contained, offering all the power and convenience of a smartphone in a lightweight, wearable format.

Ultimately, the question of whether **Orion** can truly replace smartphones comes down to balancing **power, portability, and convenience**. Right now, the limitations of battery life and the need for an external computing unit prevent it from fully competing with smartphones, which offer an all-in-one solution that's hard to beat. However, with ongoing advancements in both hardware and software, Orion has the potential to evolve into a more **self-contained, efficient device** that could eventually take the place of smartphones in our daily lives.

In the meantime, **Orion** represents an exciting step forward in the world of augmented reality. While it may not yet be the perfect smartphone replacement, it shows us a glimpse of what's possible as technology continues to advance. With future iterations likely to bring **improved battery life**, more **integrated components**, and greater **convenience**, Meta's vision for Orion as a **revolutionary AR device** is not far from becoming a reality.

The key will be finding the right balance between power and portability, ensuring that the glasses can offer all the functionality of a smartphone while remaining light, comfortable, and convenient enough for everyday use.

Chapter 7: Privacy and Security: The Double-Edged Sword of AR Glasses

The rapid advancement of **augmented reality (AR) technology** brings exciting possibilities for how we interact with the world, but it also introduces complex challenges—chief among them, **privacy and security**. With devices like Meta's Orion Smart Glasses, which are designed to **constantly monitor their surroundings** to deliver real-time information, privacy concerns become unavoidable. These glasses are equipped with cameras, microphones, and sensors that continually capture data from the user's environment.

While this is necessary to provide the immersive AR experience that makes Orion so groundbreaking, it also raises serious questions about how much of our personal and public lives are being recorded, analyzed, and potentially shared without our consent.

The first major concern with AR devices like Orion is their capacity to **record everything happening around them**. Unlike smartphones, where users typically have to manually activate the camera or microphone, AR glasses are often on and collecting data in the background. This constant surveillance has privacy advocates worried, particularly about the **unintended capture of bystanders** who may not even realize they're being filmed.

For example, if someone wearing Orion is walking through a crowded city or sitting in a café, the cameras and microphones are actively capturing the environment, including conversations and activities of people nearby. This raises serious questions about **informed consent**—how do you ensure that everyone being recorded is aware of it and has given their permission?

In addition to bystander concerns, **personal privacy** for the users themselves becomes a critical issue. Since Orion integrates with **Meta AI**, it's capable of tracking an individual's activities, preferences, and interactions in real-time. This means the device knows where you are, what you're doing, and potentially even what you're looking at. The sheer volume of data that AR devices can collect is unprecedented, from location information to real-world interactions, and how this data is stored, used, and protected is a legitimate worry for users.

Given that AR glasses are expected to be worn for long periods throughout the day, this data collection could provide an incredibly detailed **digital footprint** of a person's daily life, raising concerns about **surveillance** and potential misuse of that data.

To address these concerns, **Meta has pledged to implement strict privacy measures** for Orion.

The company has emphasized that **user privacy** is a top priority and has outlined several strategies to **protect sensitive data**. One of the most important steps Meta plans to take is the **encryption of data**, ensuring that any information collected by Orion is securely stored and only accessible by authorized parties. Meta also aims to give users **greater control** over what data is collected and how it is used, offering customizable settings that allow individuals to disable certain features, such as location tracking or voice command history. By giving users more control over their data, Meta hopes to ease concerns about surveillance and ensure that Orion is seen as a safe and secure device.

However, despite these promises, **Meta's track record with privacy** is far from perfect, and this could impact consumer trust in Orion. The company has been at the center of several major **privacy scandals** in recent years, most notably the **Cambridge Analytica** scandal, where the data of millions of Facebook users was harvested without their consent and used for political purposes.

This and other incidents have tarnished Meta's reputation when it comes to data privacy, leading to widespread skepticism about whether the company can be trusted to handle sensitive information responsibly. For potential Orion users, this history may raise red flags, especially given the even more personal nature of the data that AR glasses could collect.

Beyond specific incidents, **Meta's overall business model**, which is largely based on the collection and monetization of user data, adds to the concern. There is a fear that the data collected by Orion could be used not just for improving user experiences but for more invasive purposes, such as targeted advertising or behavioral profiling.

For example, if Meta were to analyze the data gathered by Orion's cameras and sensors, it could potentially build detailed profiles of users' habits, preferences, and movements, which could then be sold to advertisers or other third parties. This level of **data commercialization** would likely be viewed as a major breach of trust by users who expect their personal information to be protected.

Despite these risks, **Meta is making efforts to regain consumer trust** by being more transparent about its data practices. The company has promised to offer **clear disclosures** about how data is collected, who has access to it, and what it is being used for. Additionally, Meta has committed to working with **third-party auditors** to ensure that its privacy policies are being followed and that user data is being handled responsibly.

These steps are designed to reassure potential users that Meta is serious about privacy and is taking meaningful actions to protect their information. However, whether these efforts will be enough to overcome the lingering distrust from past controversies remains to be seen.

The broader issue of privacy and security with AR devices like Orion also relates to the **potential risks and benefits of always-on technology** in daily life. On the one hand, having a device that constantly monitors your environment and provides real-time information can be incredibly useful. It allows for hands-free interaction with digital content, instant access to information, and enhanced situational awareness, making tasks like navigation, communication, and learning more efficient and seamless.

For instance, **real-time object identification** could provide valuable assistance in education, allowing students to learn about their surroundings interactively, or in healthcare, where doctors could use AR to access patient information without interrupting their workflow.

On the other hand, the very feature that makes AR glasses so powerful—**their ability to constantly monitor the world around them**—is also their greatest privacy threat. In a world where everyone is wearing AR glasses, we could potentially be under **constant surveillance**, both from the companies that manufacture the devices and from each other. The idea of always being recorded, even passively, could fundamentally change how people behave in public and private spaces, leading to a **loss of anonymity** and an increase in self-censorship. People may feel uncomfortable knowing that their every move could be captured by someone else's glasses, leading to a shift in social dynamics and personal freedoms.

Moreover, the **ethical implications** of this constant surveillance cannot be ignored. **Who owns the data collected by AR glasses?**

Should there be restrictions on how and where these devices can be used, particularly in sensitive locations like **schools, hospitals, or private homes?** These are questions that will need to be addressed as AR technology becomes more prevalent, and it will be up to companies like Meta to establish clear **ethical guidelines** to prevent misuse.

The challenge for Meta will be finding a way to balance the incredible **potential of AR technology** with the need to protect user privacy. This will require not only strong encryption and security measures but also a **commitment to transparency** and **user control**. Ultimately, for Orion to succeed, Meta will need to prove that it can offer the benefits of always-on AR without sacrificing the **trust** and **privacy** of its users.

In conclusion, while **Orion Smart Glasses** offer exciting new possibilities for augmented reality, they also come with significant privacy and security concerns. The always-on nature of AR devices means that both users and bystanders could be constantly monitored, raising questions about consent, data protection, and surveillance.

Meta's efforts to address these concerns, through encryption, user control, and transparency, are a positive step, but the company's past controversies may make it difficult to win over skeptical consumers. As AR technology continues to develop, it will be crucial for Meta and other companies in the space to find the right balance between innovation and privacy, ensuring that the incredible potential of AR can be realized without compromising the rights and security of individuals.

Chapter 8: Competing with Giants: How Orion Stacks Up Against Apple, Microsoft, and Google

As **Meta's Orion Smart Glasses** prepare to enter the market, the competition is fierce. Tech giants like **Apple**, **Microsoft**, and **Google** are all vying for dominance in the **augmented reality (AR)** space, each with their own unique approach to the technology. Each company brings different strengths, target markets, and innovations to the table, creating a diverse landscape of AR solutions. The challenge for Orion will be to carve out its own niche in this competitive environment, offering a device that not only matches the technical sophistication of its competitors but also appeals to a wide range of consumers.

First, let's look at **Apple's Vision Pro**, which represents one of the most direct competitors to Orion. **Apple Vision Pro**, like all Apple products, is built with a heavy focus on **design, functionality, and premium user experience**.

The Vision Pro is Apple's entry into the world of **mixed reality**, blending both augmented reality (AR) and virtual reality (VR) experiences into a single device. As with all Apple products, design is paramount, and the Vision Pro reflects Apple's signature focus on creating sleek, visually appealing technology. The device features **high-end materials** and a minimalist aesthetic, which makes it more consumer-friendly in terms of appearance, a critical factor for AR glasses to be worn comfortably in public.

The Vision Pro, however, is not designed to replace smartphones but to augment certain aspects of digital life, such as immersive video calls, entertainment, and productivity tasks in a mixed-reality environment.

Functionality is another key area where Apple's Vision Pro shines. It incorporates **high-resolution displays**, advanced sensors, and cutting-edge computing power to deliver a truly immersive experience. Apple has also heavily focused on the **user interface**, ensuring that interactions with digital content feel natural and intuitive. Much like Meta's Orion, Vision Pro supports **gesture control** and **voice commands**, although Apple's implementation may feel more polished due to the company's long history of refining user experience across its devices. Additionally, Vision Pro's ability to switch seamlessly between AR and VR environments gives it a broader range of applications, especially for creative professionals and those who need to collaborate in virtual spaces.

However, one major drawback of Apple's Vision Pro is its **pricing**. The device is expected to retail at **$3,499**, placing it firmly in the luxury tech category. This makes it inaccessible to most mainstream consumers, especially when compared to more affordable tech like smartphones and tablets.

Apple is clearly positioning the Vision Pro as a **premium product** for early adopters, creative professionals, and tech enthusiasts, rather than a device aimed at mass-market adoption. This leaves room for **Meta's Orion** to potentially capture a broader audience by offering a more **affordable** and accessible AR experience, especially if Meta can successfully bridge the gap between consumer and enterprise markets.

Speaking of **enterprise markets**, **Microsoft** has taken a very different approach to AR with its **HoloLens** series. **Microsoft HoloLens** has been on the market for several years and is primarily focused on **enterprise use** rather than the consumer market. HoloLens is designed for specialized applications in industries such as healthcare, engineering, and education. It enables professionals to interact with 3D models, collaborate remotely in virtual environments, and access complex data in real-time while working hands-free. The **enterprise focus** has allowed Microsoft to build a solid user base in fields where AR technology can provide clear, immediate value, such as industrial design, remote training, and even surgery.

One of the strengths of **HoloLens** is its **robust functionality** for enterprise tasks, but it comes at the cost of accessibility for everyday consumers. The device is larger and bulkier than consumer-oriented AR glasses like Orion and Vision Pro, and its price tag—over **$3,500**—also reflects its professional target audience. Additionally, **HoloLens** has focused heavily on **virtual collaboration** and **industrial applications**, meaning that it's less suited for casual use or entertainment compared to Meta's vision for Orion.

However, Microsoft's **early start in the AR space** and its focus on real-world enterprise applications give it a competitive advantage in these specialized markets, where **functionality** and **precision** are more important than design or mass-market appeal.

Then there's **Google**, another giant in the tech world that has had a rocky journey with AR technology. Google's initial foray into AR with **Google Glass** was ambitious but ultimately unsuccessful, largely due to concerns over **privacy**, **design flaws**, and the device's awkward, early-adopter appearance. Despite these setbacks, **Google** has not given up on AR and has since shifted its focus toward **enterprise AR solutions**.

Google Glass is still used in industries like manufacturing and healthcare, where hands-free access to information can enhance productivity and safety. Google has also made significant investments in **AR development**

tools, such as **ARCore**, which helps developers create AR apps for Android devices.

Google's current strategy seems less focused on building a standalone consumer AR device and more on **supporting AR development** across a variety of platforms. This gives Meta's Orion an opportunity to stand out in the consumer AR market, as Google's pivot away from consumer products leaves a gap that Orion could fill. Additionally, Meta's ownership of the world's largest social media platforms—Facebook, Instagram, and WhatsApp—gives Orion a unique **advantage** that neither Google nor Microsoft can match: **social media integration**.

This brings us to one of Meta's key advantages in the AR race: its **social media dominance**. Orion could leverage Meta's vast ecosystem to offer features that none of its competitors can easily replicate. **Hands-free browsing, messaging**, and **social media interaction** are all natural extensions of Meta's platforms, and Orion could seamlessly integrate these features into its AR interface. Imagine being able to scroll through your Instagram feed, respond to Facebook messages, or even make WhatsApp video calls—all without touching your phone. This level of **social integration** is a unique selling point that could make Orion especially appealing to younger consumers and those who are already deeply embedded in Meta's social media ecosystem.

By leveraging its **social media networks**, Meta can also offer exclusive AR experiences that tie into users' online identities. For instance, users could receive **augmented reality notifications** when they get a message or alert, or they could participate in **immersive social media experiences**, such as attending virtual events or interacting with 3D avatars of their friends.

This gives Orion a distinct edge over competitors like Apple and Microsoft, which, while technologically advanced, lack the built-in social network infrastructure to offer such a connected experience.

Meta's opportunity to **bridge the gap** between **consumer appeal** and **enterprise-level functionality** is another area where Orion could excel. While Apple's Vision Pro and Microsoft's HoloLens are targeted at different ends of the AR spectrum—one aimed at high-end consumers and creatives, the other at professionals in specialized fields—Meta is positioning Orion to appeal to both audiences. With **Meta AI integration**, hands-free social media interactions, and **immersive AR experiences**, Orion is designed to be both practical for professional use and fun for everyday consumers.

In conclusion, Meta's **Orion Smart Glasses** face stiff competition from tech giants like Apple, Microsoft, and Google, each of whom has carved out a unique space in the AR market. **Apple's Vision Pro** excels in design and user experience but comes with a hefty price tag that limits its mass appeal. **Microsoft's HoloLens** dominates the enterprise market with specialized applications but is less accessible for everyday consumers.

Google, meanwhile, has shifted its focus toward enterprise and AR development tools, leaving an opportunity for Orion to capture the consumer AR market. Meta's ability to leverage its social media platforms, offer hands-free browsing and messaging, and create a bridge between consumer and enterprise functionality gives Orion a strong position in this competitive landscape. Whether it can fully capitalize on these advantages will depend on its pricing, design, and ability to deliver a seamless, immersive AR experience that appeals to a wide range of users.

Chapter 9: Beyond the Consumer Market: Orion's Potential in Industry and Education

Meta's Orion Smart Glasses may be positioned as a consumer-friendly augmented reality (AR) device, but their potential extends far beyond everyday use. The capabilities of AR glasses, such as real-time object recognition, data overlay, and hands-free interaction, have the power to revolutionize a wide array of **industries**. Sectors like **healthcare, education, and entertainment** are already exploring AR's transformative potential, and Orion could become a key player in this shift.

By offering features that can streamline processes, enhance learning, and deliver new forms of entertainment, Orion has the potential to impact **enterprises** in ways that go well beyond consumer use.

In **healthcare**, AR glasses could radically transform how medical professionals operate. Imagine a surgeon wearing Orion during a complex procedure, with real-time data and imaging overlaid directly into their field of vision.

Instead of constantly looking at monitors or reference materials, the surgeon could see crucial information, such as a patient's vitals, 3D scans, or even guidance from AI-powered tools, without diverting their eyes from the task at hand. This kind of **hands-free access to information** could improve accuracy, reduce errors, and ultimately lead to better patient outcomes. Additionally, Orion could be used for **remote consultations**, allowing specialists to assist or guide procedures from afar by seeing exactly what the on-site doctor sees through the AR interface.

The **potential for training and education** within healthcare is also immense. Medical students could use Orion to practice surgeries or other procedures in a controlled AR environment, receiving guidance and feedback in real-time as they work through simulations.

This offers a **safe, immersive training experience** that can supplement traditional learning, helping students gain confidence and experience without putting actual patients at risk. The ability to visualize complex anatomical structures in 3D could also aid in teaching, making it easier for students to understand difficult concepts or processes.

Education is another field that stands to gain enormously from the integration of AR technology. Classrooms equipped with AR glasses like Orion could offer students a more **interactive and engaging learning experience**. Instead of learning solely through textbooks and static images, students could explore 3D models of historical events, scientific processes, or geographic locations, all within their classroom environment.

For instance, history students could witness a **battle reenactment** overlaid onto the school grounds, or biology students could explore the inner workings of a cell in stunning detail, with labels and explanations provided in real time as they move through the digital scene. This kind of **immersive learning** could not only make lessons more engaging but also cater to **different learning styles**, allowing students to grasp complex concepts through visual and experiential means.

Orion could also help foster **collaboration** in educational settings. Teachers and students could work together on AR projects, sharing real-time data and interactive experiences, regardless of their physical location. This would be particularly valuable in **distance learning** scenarios, where students and teachers are separated by geography. With Orion, students could still feel as if they're present in the same classroom, participating in interactive lessons and activities, even if they're miles apart. This kind of **remote learning** could provide a richer, more connected experience than traditional video conferencing tools alone, allowing students to remain engaged in their learning regardless of where they are.

In the **entertainment industry**, AR glasses have the potential to create entirely new forms of immersive experiences. For example, **gaming** could be taken to new heights, with Orion offering players the ability to interact with their environment in ways that go beyond traditional screens. AR games that take place in the real world, with digital elements overlaid onto physical spaces, could provide an unparalleled sense of **immersion and engagement**.

Imagine walking through your own home or city, with digital characters, puzzles, and challenges appearing in real-time as you move. Orion could also be used in **theaters and live performances**, where audiences could experience augmented versions of the show, with digital effects, interactive elements, or additional information overlaid onto the stage or performers.

Beyond gaming and live entertainment, AR glasses like Orion could also revolutionize the **film industry**. Directors, set designers, and other creative professionals could use Orion to visualize scenes, props, or special effects in real-time before filming. This would allow for **better planning and creative control**, as filmmakers could see how different elements will look in a scene without needing to rely solely on imagination or post-production. For audiences, Orion could offer a more interactive viewing experience, where movies or TV shows include AR elements that expand the story beyond the screen, inviting viewers to become more active participants in the narrative.

Another key area where Orion could make an impact is in **creative industries** like architecture, design, and art.

Architects, for instance, could use AR to visualize buildings and structures in real-world settings before they're constructed. With Orion, a designer could walk through an empty lot and see a **full-scale digital model** of a building overlaid onto the space, allowing them to make real-time adjustments and see how the structure fits into its environment. This kind of **real-world visualization** could save time, reduce costs, and help avoid potential design flaws early in the planning stages.

Art and design could also be transformed by AR. Artists and designers could create **interactive digital works** that blend seamlessly into the physical world, allowing viewers to engage with the artwork in new ways. This could open up entirely new forms of creative expression, where art is no longer confined to a static medium but can change, evolve, and interact with its environment.

Orion's ability to **overlay digital elements onto the real world** could inspire new forms of creativity that we can only begin to imagine.

Orion's potential is not just limited to creative and educational fields. **Enterprises** across various industries are already exploring AR technology to **enhance productivity and efficiency**, and Meta's glasses could be a key tool in this transformation. For example, in **manufacturing**, AR glasses can provide workers with real-time instructions, allowing them to assemble complex machinery or perform repairs without needing to refer to manuals or instructions on a screen.

Instead, step-by-step guides and interactive 3D models can be projected directly into the worker's field of vision, streamlining the process and reducing errors. Similarly, in **logistics**, AR could help workers navigate large warehouses or find products faster by overlaying digital directions or inventory information onto the physical space.

For companies involved in **field services**, AR glasses could provide workers with hands-free access to important data while they're on the job. A technician repairing a piece of equipment in a remote location could use Orion to receive remote support from an expert, who could see exactly what the technician is looking at and offer guidance in real-time. This kind of **remote collaboration** could reduce the need for travel, save time, and improve the quality of service provided.

Orion's entry into the enterprise market could also have a significant impact on **sectors that have already begun exploring AR technology**, such as **retail** and **hospitality**. In retail, AR glasses could offer new ways for customers to engage with products, from trying on virtual clothing to seeing how furniture might look in their home.

In hospitality, AR could enhance guest experiences by offering interactive tours, personalized recommendations, or real-time translations in different languages.

In summary, while **Meta's Orion Smart Glasses** are designed with consumers in mind, their potential extends far beyond the consumer market. Industries like **healthcare, education, entertainment**, and various **enterprises** are already beginning to explore how AR technology can enhance their operations, improve training, and create more engaging experiences. Orion's ability to offer **hands-free access to real-time data**, **immersive learning environments**, and **interactive digital content** could transform how these sectors operate.

Whether in the classroom, hospital, or creative studio, the potential for Orion to become an indispensable tool in **professional and educational settings** is enormous, and its impact on these industries could be profound. As more companies and institutions adopt AR technology, Orion could play a central role in driving innovation and shaping the future of work, learning, and entertainment.

Chapter 10: The Future of Smart Glasses: Where Do We Go from Here?

As **Meta's Orion Smart Glasses** continue to generate excitement, one of the key questions on everyone's mind is: **When will they be available for consumers?** While Meta has yet to announce an official release date, industry insiders predict that the first consumer version of Orion could be released **around 2027,** based on Meta's current development timeline. The first iteration of Orion is expected to offer a mix of high-tech features, including **advanced augmented reality (AR)** capabilities, gesture control through the **EMG wristband**, and **Meta AI integration** for voice commands and real-time contextual information.

However, like many emerging technologies, the early versions of Orion may come with limitations, particularly in terms of battery life, cost, and overall refinement. The real question is: **What will the future of AR glasses look like beyond the first release**, and how might these devices evolve to become essential tools in our daily lives?

One of the biggest areas where **AR glasses** are expected to improve in the coming years is **battery life**. Currently, the challenge for most AR devices, including Orion, is balancing performance with power consumption. High-resolution displays, real-time tracking, and constant data processing require significant energy, and early versions of Orion are likely to have **limited battery life**—perhaps lasting only a few hours of intensive use before needing a recharge.

However, as **battery technology** continues to advance, we can expect AR glasses to become more efficient, offering **longer-lasting**

power without compromising on functionality. Innovations in **solid-state batteries**, for example, could dramatically increase battery life while reducing the size and weight of the battery itself, making future versions of Orion more practical for all-day wear.

Another critical area for improvement is **miniaturization**. While the first versions of Orion are expected to be lighter and sleeker than earlier AR devices like **Magic Leap** or **Microsoft's HoloLens**, they will still likely feature **visible tech elements**, such as thicker frames to house the necessary sensors, cameras, and display components. As AR technology evolves, we can expect these components to become smaller and more discreet, allowing AR glasses to **look and feel more like regular eyewear**.

The goal for Meta—and indeed for the entire AR industry—is to create glasses that are **indistinguishable** from the ones we wear today, blending seamlessly into everyday fashion while offering cutting-edge AR functionality. This kind of **miniaturization** will be essential for widespread consumer adoption, as many potential users may be hesitant to wear visibly bulky or high-tech glasses in public.

Cost will also be a significant factor in the evolution of AR glasses. Early versions of Orion, like many emerging technologies, are expected to carry a **premium price tag**, likely in the same range as **Apple's Vision Pro**, which is priced at $3,499. This high cost will limit initial adoption to early adopters and tech enthusiasts, but as the technology matures and **production scales**, the price of AR glasses is expected to **decrease**.

Much like smartphones, which were once considered luxury items but are now ubiquitous, AR glasses have the potential to **become more affordable** over time, eventually reaching a price point that makes them accessible to the mass market. As costs come down and features improve, AR glasses could transform from niche gadgets into everyday essentials for millions of people around the world.

So, how could **AR glasses** like Orion transform from being **niche products** into **everyday essentials**? The key lies in their potential to replace many of the devices we currently rely on, particularly **smartphones**. Today, smartphones are our primary tools for communication, entertainment, navigation, and productivity. However, the vision behind AR glasses is that they could one day **replace smartphones entirely**, offering a more immersive, hands-free way to interact with the digital world.

With Orion, users could make calls, send messages, browse the web, and even interact with social media—all without needing to pull out their phones. Navigation could be overlaid directly onto the streets in front of you, messages could appear as holograms in your field of vision, and video calls could feel more immersive than ever before, with the person you're speaking to appearing as a hologram in your environment.

In this vision of the future, **AR glasses** would become the primary way we access digital information, freeing us from the need to constantly check our phones. This shift could dramatically change how we interact with technology in our daily lives, making it more integrated and less intrusive. Instead of staring at screens, we would interact with digital content naturally as it appears in our field of vision, allowing us to stay more present in the real world. For many, this would represent a **paradigm shift** in how we experience technology, making it more fluid, accessible, and adaptable to our needs.

However, there are significant challenges to this vision. While **Meta** has ambitious plans for Orion and the future of AR, there are still

technical and societal hurdles to overcome before AR glasses can truly replace smartphones.

First, there's the issue of **privacy**. As discussed earlier, AR glasses that are always on and constantly collecting data about the environment could raise serious concerns about **surveillance** and **data security**. For AR glasses to become everyday tools, companies like Meta will need to address these concerns head-on, ensuring that users feel their **personal data** is safe and that they have control over what information is collected and how it's used.

Another challenge is **user acceptance**. While early adopters and tech enthusiasts may be excited about the potential of AR glasses, convincing the broader public to embrace this new technology will take time. Many people are still attached to their smartphones and may be hesitant to adopt a new device that feels unfamiliar or too high-tech.

Cultural shifts in how we use and perceive technology will be necessary for AR glasses to become as essential as smartphones are today. This could take years, if not decades, as society gradually adapts to the idea of wearing technology on our faces instead of holding it in our hands.

Furthermore, the **ecosystem** of apps and services for AR glasses will need to grow and mature. Much like the early days of smartphones, where app developers needed time to create innovative and useful applications, the AR glasses market will require a robust ecosystem of **AR-specific apps** to make the device truly valuable. Meta's integration with its social media platforms like **Facebook, Instagram, and WhatsApp** will give Orion a head start in offering compelling use cases, such as **hands-free browsing** and **immersive social media experiences**, but more will be needed to fully replace the functionality of smartphones.

Despite these challenges, **Meta's vision** for a world where **AR glasses** replace smartphones is not out of reach.

As AR technology continues to improve, and as companies like Meta, Apple, and Microsoft pour resources into developing **smaller, more powerful, and more affordable AR devices**, it's entirely possible that AR glasses could become the dominant form of personal technology in the coming decades. The transition from smartphones to AR glasses may not happen overnight, but as the technology matures, the benefits of **hands-free, immersive computing** will likely become too compelling to ignore.

In this future, **Meta's Orion Smart Glasses** could play a leading role in **redefining personal technology**. By offering a device that combines cutting-edge AR capabilities with **social media integration, hands-free interaction,** and **AI-driven assistance**, Meta has positioned Orion as more than just a gadget—it's a glimpse into the future of how we'll interact with the digital world. While the road to full smartphone replacement may be long, Orion is a crucial step in that direction, and as the technology continues to evolve, the future of **smart glasses** looks brighter than ever.

In conclusion, the future of **AR glasses** is filled with exciting possibilities, from extended battery life and miniaturization to lower costs and broader consumer adoption. Meta's Orion has the potential to be a **game-changer** in this space, but the journey to replacing smartphones with AR glasses will require continued innovation, cultural shifts, and advancements in both technology and privacy.

Whether it's in the next five or ten years, the day when AR glasses become a ubiquitous part of our daily lives is on the horizon, and Meta's Orion may be at the forefront of this transformation.

CONCLUSION

The Beginning of a New Era

Meta's Orion Smart Glasses represent the beginning of a **new era** in how we interact with technology. With its powerful **augmented reality (AR) capabilities**, **gesture control** via the **EMG wristband**, and **Meta AI integration**, Orion offers a vision of the future where digital content is seamlessly overlaid onto the real world, creating a more immersive and hands-free experience than ever before. Unlike smartphones, which require constant physical interaction, Orion allows users to engage with information, apps, and social media without lifting a finger.

From **real-time navigation** and **voice commands** to **social media integration** and **object identification**, Orion's potential to transform how we communicate, learn, work, and entertain ourselves is immense.

What makes **Orion different** from its predecessors and competitors is its focus on balancing advanced **AR technology** with practical, everyday use. Earlier AR devices like **Google Glass**, **Microsoft HoloLens**, and **Magic Leap** each had their limitations—whether it was bulky design, high cost, or narrow application scope. **Orion**, however, combines a more **refined design** with a broader appeal. It aims to bridge the gap between **consumer-friendly wearability** and **enterprise-level functionality**, making it not just a tool for professionals but a device that could be worn and used by anyone.

While competitors like **Apple's Vision Pro** and **Microsoft's HoloLens** offer impressive technology, they remain focused on niche markets—either as high-end luxury products or specialized enterprise tools. Orion's focus on **social media integration, hands-free** browsing, and **personalized AI assistance** sets it apart by making AR feel more accessible and relevant to a wider audience.

Yet, the road ahead for **AR glasses** like Orion is not without its challenges. One of the key questions is how long it will take before **AR glasses are widely adopted** and whether they can realistically **replace smartphones**. Currently, there are still hurdles in terms of **battery life, miniaturization, pricing,** and **user acceptance.** Early versions of Orion, while innovative, may face limitations that prevent them from becoming mainstream devices in the near term. However, as AR technology continues to improve—particularly in areas like **battery efficiency** and **component miniaturization**—we can expect AR glasses to become lighter, more powerful, and more affordable, making them increasingly attractive to everyday users.

The shift from **smartphones to AR glasses** will not happen overnight. Smartphones have become deeply embedded in our lives, offering an all-in-one solution that's hard to beat. However, the potential for **AR glasses** to eventually replace smartphones is real.

Imagine a world where your **hands-free AR device** gives you access to everything your smartphone does, but in a more natural, immersive way—whether it's overlaying navigation onto the streets in front of you, displaying messages in your field of vision, or allowing you to interact with friends through **augmented social media experiences**. The transition will be gradual, but as the technology becomes more refined and as **cultural attitudes shift**, AR glasses could eventually become the **dominant form of personal technology**.

So, will **Orion** succeed in its mission to lead this new era of **AR technology**? The answer depends on several factors. Meta's ability to address concerns around **privacy**, **data**

security, and **pricing** will be crucial in gaining widespread consumer trust.

Additionally, as the technology advances, Meta must continue to innovate, offering not only improved hardware but also a **robust ecosystem of apps** and services that make AR indispensable. Given Meta's unique position as a **social media giant**, the company has an edge in offering **connected, social experiences** that could drive the adoption of Orion among consumers who are already familiar with its platforms like **Facebook, Instagram,** and **WhatsApp**.

In the end, **Orion** represents more than just a new gadget—it's a glimpse into the **digital future** where the boundaries between the physical and virtual worlds blur, and **augmented reality** becomes an integral part of how we live, work, and play. As AR glasses continue to evolve and become more **affordable** and **integrated** into our daily lives, Meta's vision of a world where AR replaces smartphones may not be far off. While there are still challenges to overcome, the introduction of Orion marks the beginning of a **new era** in **personal technology**, and its impact will likely shape the digital landscape for years to come.

www.ingramcontent.com/pod-product-compliance
Lightning Source LLC
Chambersburg PA
CBHW071100240526
45471CB00016B/2255